Essential Tru
Principals

School principals are constantly being pulled in different directions. How do you focus on the things that matter most? In this inspiring book from Danny Steele, creator of the popular Steele Thoughts blog, and Todd Whitaker, bestselling author and speaker, you'll learn how to center your leadership on your core values and the practices that have the biggest impact. The authors reveal essential truths that will make you a more effective principal in areas such as school culture, appreciating teachers, and empowering your staff. The strategies are presented in digestible chunks, perfect for book studies, professional development sessions, and other learning formats. With the inspiring anecdotes and insights in this book, you'll be reminded of your greater purpose – making a difference in students' lives.

Danny Steele (@steelethoughts) is a principal from Birmingham, Alabama, and has worked in public education for over 25 years. In 2016, he was named Alabama's Secondary Principal of the Year. He has presented at numerous state and national conferences, and he serves as an adjunct instructor at the University of Montevallo. Danny writes an educational leadership blog that has received over 5 million page views.

Todd Whitaker (@toddwhitaker) is a professor of educational leadership at the University of Missouri. He is a leading presenter in the field of education and has written more than 50 books, including the national bestsellers *What Great Teachers Do Differently* and *Your First Year: How to Survive and Thrive as a New Teacher*, co-written with Madeline Whitaker Good and Katherine Whitaker.

THE Best Mission statements
are not framed they are lived

Parent send us the best children they
ave ; they do the best they know how

we always need to look for the good part
Even if we have to squint

Essential Truths for Principals

Danny Steele and Todd Whitaker

Routledge
Taylor & Francis Group

NEW YORK AND LONDON

First published 2019
by Routledge
52 Vanderbilt Avenue, New York, NY 10017

and by Routledge
2 Park Square, Milton Park, Abingdon, Oxon, OX14 4RN

Routledge is an imprint of the Taylor & Francis Group, an informa business

Library of Congress Cataloging-in-Publication Data
Names: Steele, Danny, author. | Whitaker, Todd, 1959- author.
Title: Essential truths for principals / Danny Steele and Todd Whitaker.
Description: New York, NY : Routledge, 2019.
Identifiers: LCCN 2018044601 (print) | LCCN 2018047464 (ebook) |
ISBN 9780429028649 (ebook) | ISBN 9780367137991 (hardback) | ISBN
9780367138011 (pbk.)
Subjects: LCSH: School principals–Professional relationships. |
Educational leadership. | School environment. | Home and school.
Classification: LCC LB2831.9 (ebook) | LCC LB2831.9 .S73 2019 (print) |
DDC 371.2/012–dc23
LC record available at https://lccn.loc.gov/2018044601

ISBN: 978-0-367-13799-1 (hbk)
ISBN: 978-0-367-13801-1 (pbk)
ISBN: 978-0-429-02864-9 (ebk)

Typeset in Palatino
by Swales & Willis Ltd, Exeter, Devon, UK

For my wife, Holley, and kids, DJ, Will, and Elizabeth –
thank you for your constant encouragement and support.
And for my brother, David – who was talking to me
about the book I would one day write, years before it
was even a pipe dream.

Danny

This book is dedicated to our grandson, Tapley.

Todd

Contents

Meet the Authors

Dr. Danny Steele is a principal from Birmingham, Alabama, and has worked in public education for over 25 years. In addition to serving as a principal at multiple levels, he has worked as a teacher, coach, and assistant principal. In 2005, Danny was recognized as the Secondary Assistant Principal of the Year for the state of Alabama, and in 2016 he was named Alabama's Secondary Principal of the Year. He has presented at numerous state and national conferences. He serves as an adjunct instructor at the University of Montevallo (AL), and writes an educational leadership blog that has received over 5 million page views. Danny has an undergraduate degree in History from Covenant College (Lookout Mountain, GA); he has an M.A. in History from the University of Alabama (Birmingham); he has an Educational Specialist degree in Educational Administration and an Educational Doctorate degree in Educational Leadership – both from Samford University (Birmingham, AL). He lives with his wife, Holley, in Birmingham, Alabama. They have three children: DJ, Will, and Elizabeth.

Dr. Todd Whitaker is a professor of educational leadership at the University of Missouri, Columbia, and professor emeritus at Indiana State University, Terre Haute. Prior to moving into higher education he was a math teacher and basketball coach in Missouri. Todd then served as a principal at the middle school, junior high, and high school levels. He was also a middle school coordinator in charge of staffing, curriculum, and technology for the opening of new middle schools. He has spent his life pursuing his love of education by researching and studying effective teachers and principals.

One of the nation's leading authorities on staff motivation, leading change, and teacher and principal effectiveness, Todd has written over 50 books including the national bestseller, *What Great Teachers Do Differently*. Other titles include: *Your First Year, Shifting The Monkey, Dealing With Difficult Teachers, The Ten-Minute Inservice, The Ball, What Great Principals Do Differently, Motivating & Inspiring Teachers,* and *Dealing With Difficult Parents*.

Todd is married to Beth, also a former teacher and principal, who is a professor of Educational Leadership at the University of Missouri. They are the parents of three children: Katherine, Madeline, and Harrison.

Preface

Everything comes down to leadership. When things are going well in a school it comes down to the leader. When things are not going so well in a school it comes down to the leader. Principals are pulled in many directions. There are never-ending expectations and demands from: students, teachers, and staff members within a school; outside influences such as parents and community members; and demands and expectations from central office leaders. How we decide what to emphasize and how to balance all of these tugs and pulls will determine the impact we have on our school, staff, and students.

This book is designed to help us continue to center our leadership on the things that matter the most. And by doing so it allows everyone involved with our school to consistently focus on the people that matter the most – the students. Principals have to take care of their teachers so that the teachers can take care of the students. Making sure we value, cultivate, and celebrate our teachers is an essential component of being the principal our school needs.

Programs and initiatives come and go so regularly in education that it becomes difficult to determine what to focus on next. Seemingly every year/month/week/day there are increasing demands on educators to do the next "great" thing that will change the world. Some of these things are positive and others not so much. Amazingly, many of them – and even some of the positive ones – tend to disappear into the air like a fine mist. What was labeled as the most important thing in the world disappears into an afterthought. This revolving door of change can result in a furrowed brow or a cynical frown at what comes next. It is so easy to feel the demands and pressures of standardized testing, increasing accountability, and expanding expectations on all of us. It is easy to fall into the "what's next" trap or even the "is it all worth it?" mind set. This is quite natural as the pressure continues to mount. It may even lead to hopelessness. Is there nothing that is constant that we can rely on for guidance? Are we just continually adrift at sea, eyeing the next storm?

The purpose of this book is to determine the timeless things that have always worked and will always work. Then we must remember to emphasize and implement these practices every day. It is exciting to have a fun first day of school. Teacher of the year recognition banquets can be a fitting celebration of educators. But there are plenty of days in between, and the things we do every day, consistently, to build a depth of trust, morale, and self-worth are what separates the best principals from all of the rest. Leadership is not an event.

Despite the changes that are occurring like a whipsaw, there are some constants that effective leaders know have a more permanent shelf life. There are things that provide an impact whether we work at a preschool, high school, or anywhere in between. Rather than trying to do the current things, we must all strive to do the important things.

Whether we are in our first year or forty-first year we all want to make a difference. That's why we chose education. Typically, we started in the classroom and loved it. We taught to influence and improve the lives of our students. But then we realized we wanted to increase our impact and expand our influence. That is why we chose to lead. This is our chance. Educational leaders are at their best when they operate from their core – when they go through their day, mindful of the values that drive them. Whether this book alters the path you are on or gives you the confidence to accelerate on your current road, our purpose is to remind us why we chose education and to become a leader that affects the future.

How to Use This Book

Our goal is to provide a book that you can use when you most need it. You can sit down and devour it like a traditional book, front-to-back. You might want to highlight or dog-ear parts that resonate for later reading. Maybe you want to start off your Monday, or every day, looking for a new idea or much-needed reminder. Maybe it is a book you want to share with your colleagues or faculty. Maybe you can reflect on a quote at the beginning of a faculty meeting or share a thought in your weekly memo. There is no limit to the possibilities.

But the real purpose of this book is to make a difference – to help us remember why we chose education and to align our long-held beliefs with our current practices. There are many things in education we cannot control. However, there are many things that we *can* control every day. Let's get started.

Essential Truths

1

Instructional Leadership Is Not About Improving Teachers; It Is About Creating the Conditions Where Teachers Can Improve Themselves.

Being the "instructional leader" of the school is probably at the top of every principal's job description. It is a nebulous concept, but it suggests to many administrators that they need to be experts on curriculum development, pedagogy, professional development, the integration of technology, and the research-based best practices that pour out of the literature and out of the workshops. That is a lot of pressure on any school leader.

Instructional leadership is not about *being* an expert, though; it is about cultivating the expertise in your building. It is about creating a culture of collaboration where teachers learn from one another and inspire one another. It is not about having all the answers; it is about asking some really good questions. It is about empowering teachers to pursue solutions to instructional problems. It is about removing barriers in the classroom. (And your

> **"** It is not about having all the answers; it is about asking some really good questions. **"**

teachers will let you know what those barriers are!) It is about providing resources that teachers need to be more effective. It is about providing a consistent focus in the building – a focus that reminds teachers why they come to work each day. It is a focus that motivates teachers to pursue excellence in the classroom. Teaching is hard work, and when it is done right can be absolutely draining. It is imperative that school leaders provide support and encouragement all year long. A principal's instructional leadership is only as strong as their commitment to supporting teachers.

2

If You Want to Evaluate a School's Culture Do Not Read the Mission Statement on the Wall, Listen to the Teachers Talk in the Hallway.

You can learn a lot about a school simply by listening to the teachers talk. Are they complaining to each other about the students' behavior or are they sharing accomplishments of their classes? Are they griping about the students who are not turning in their homework, or are they collaborating about instructional strategies? Are they counting down the days until the next break or are they smiling, laughing, and having fun with each other? The interactions of the adults in the building provide a great gauge of the culture of the building. And if you want to see a teacher's rapport with students, watch them interact with the students in the hallway. Those interactions speak volumes! Every school has basically the same mission: "Preparing kids for their future." What matters is not the quality of words in a frame, but the quality of relationships in the building.

3

Administrators Want Their Teachers to Be Sensitive to the Home Life of Students. And Administrators Need to Be Sensitive to the Home Life of Their Teachers.

There are teachers who are going through divorce. There are teachers who are battling depression. There are teachers who are coping with family illness. Teachers deal with the same stresses that affect everyone else. Teachers are professionals, and they try to be strong for their students. They continue to do their jobs with excellence. But these stresses have an impact. Teachers are human. It is imperative that school leaders recognize the reality of the stress that many of their teachers are under. Maslow's Hierarchy of Needs does not just apply to students; it applies to teachers as well. They are in the pyramid too. Principals and other administrators are more effective when they are mindful of that reality. The sensitivity, patience, and compassion of principals can go a long way to maintaining the morale and energy of these teachers. And it helps to create the sort of culture that all employees appreciate.

4

No Program in the School Will Ever Exceed the Passion of the Adults Implementing It.

I remember when our school started "Homework Cafe." We intended this to be a place for students to complete their homework during lunch if they had not finished it for their class. We know that assigning zeros was not constructive, and we did not want students to leave their assignment unfinished. We knew that this initiative would only be successful if we recruited the right staff member to supervise it. When discussing this with my assistant principal, we knew that we needed someone who would connect well with the students in the Cafe. We needed a teacher who was patient and compassionate. We needed a teacher who would be invested in the success of Homework Cafe.

Several years ago, our school launched co-curricular clubs for our students. Every student was allowed to pick a club that they were interested in, and we developed a schedule where students would meet in their clubs once or twice a month during the school day. The most important part of this process was when we asked teachers to choose a club that they would lead. I asked teachers to think of a club that they could be passionate about – a club that they would be excited about leading. Our clubs have been successful for a few years now, and we continually remind our teachers that they are the reason for the success. Their enthusiasm, dedication, and preparation are the reasons these clubs are meaningful for the students.

It does not matter what programs are going on in your school. The success of these programs will depend on the adults who are leading them. Ultimately, schools do not thrive because of programs; they thrive because of the passionate educators in the building. The adults are always the most important variable in the success of any endeavor.

> **"** Schools do not thrive because of programs; they thrive because of the passionate educators in the building. **"**

5

School Culture Is Made in the Little Moments. And We All Have Those Little Moments Where We Can Make a Difference – Every Day.

Principals shape school culture ... as do custodians, secretaries, counselors, teachers, bookkeepers, librarians, paraprofessionals, maintenance technicians, resource officers, nurses, registrars, and cafeteria workers. If you work in a school, you make a difference for that school. Everyone contributes to building a strong school culture. And good culture does not result from clever programs; it is created by the adults who care about the students and the schools. It is not created through big initiatives; it is created with personal connections. It is created through taking advantage of the little opportunities to create moments of awesomeness. And if you are alert you will discover that there are opportunities to be awesome all around you – opportunities to make someone's day – opportunities to make a difference for students, and celebrate colleagues. Building strong school culture is nothing more than making the most of all those small moments.

Not long ago, I remember telling our school custodian some knock-knock jokes. She laughed ... and that made me feel good – although she may have been laughing more at my silliness than the actual humor of the jokes. But we both had fun with it that day; we both enjoyed the interaction.

I remember a day when a student stopped me as I was walking around, and said, "Hey Dr. Steele ... do you have time for a magic trick?" What principal has time for magic tricks? But I stopped ... and was thoroughly impressed with his sleight of hand.

Every morning, I am in our cafeteria, helping to supervise students eating breakfast. We have an amazing Child Nutrition Program (CNP) staff, and one of their special talents is making cinnamon rolls. I'm glad to see the lunch ladies every morning, and they seem glad to see me. Several years ago, I made a point to talk to them about how good their cinnamon rolls were. I didn't think much of the conversation at the time, but I did want them to know that I appreciated them ... and their baking talents. The next time they served cinnamon rolls, there was a treat packaged up for me in the window between the kitchen and the serving lines: My very own cinnamon roll, set aside in a container. The sticky note read, "Enjoy, Dr. Steele!" For the last several years, on days when cinnamon rolls are being served, there is a special one waiting for me in the window. If I don't see it, they will call my attention to it. What a tasty tradition!

So what do knock-knock jokes, magic tricks, and cinnamon rolls have to do with instructional leadership? What do they have to do with raising student achievement? Nothing, I suppose.

But they have everything to do with culture. They have everything to do with relationships. They have everything to do with building the type of school where students enjoy learning and adults enjoy working. And this is the kind of school where kids and staff members thrive. School culture is not about the big things; it's about the little things. It's about the thoughtful gestures ... the high-fives, the conversations with students in the hallways, and all the smiles – don't ever forget the smiles. And yes, sometimes, it's about knock-knock jokes, magic tricks, and cinnamon rolls.

6

The Formal Mission of the School is Only as Strong as the Informal Mission of the Adults Working There.

It is easy to get into a routine. We go to work every day; we teach lessons; we lead faculty meetings; we email parents; we supervise carpool ... the list goes on. We make a million decisions every day, and many of them we are barely aware of. We get bogged down in the minutiae and the mundane. So how do we rise above the "grind" and stay mindful of why we do what we do?

At the beginning of the school year, our staff members wrote their hopes for our students on the wall outside our main office. This included our teachers, paraprofessionals, custodians, maintenance technician – everyone. These hopes are not for higher test scores or less tardiness. They are not hopes for completed homework or straight "A's". They are the hopes that inspired teachers to enter the profession. They are the passions that reflect our collective desire to make a difference in the lives of our kids. They are the reasons we come to work. We also asked teachers to write their own professional oath, modeled after the Hippocratic Oath that physicians adhere to. These oaths capture the core values of the teachers and represent their professional commitments to their students and to their colleagues.

Most schools have mission statements, and I think these are a good thing. But more important are the personal mission statements of the adults in the building. It is crucial that leaders find ways to help staff members tap into their core values – to remain mindful of their purpose. After all, schools will never be defined by the mission statement on the wall; they will be defined by what actually goes on in classrooms.

7

A Leader's Vision Is Only as Strong as Their Enthusiasm for Helping Others on the Journey.

A principal's job has no inherent value. A principal's job is valuable inasmuch as they enable their teachers to be more effective. Teachers do the core business of the school, and the job of school leaders is to remove barriers from instruction and provide their teachers with the tools and resources they need to be successful. The best instructional initiatives do not count for much if the teachers are not empowered and supported by the administration to carry them out.

8

Every School Day Is Filled with Unexpected Glitches and Hiccups. The Best Leaders Respond with Poise, Perseverance, and a Positive Attitude.

The school assembly went on longer than expected and now the lunch schedule is going to be messed up. A student threw up in the hallway and the custodian is at lunch. Two substitutes did not show up and there are about 60 students unsupervised. A parent's car died in the carpool line and has caused a traffic jam. A teacher forgot to fill out her paperwork for professional leave. If you are a school administrator, you have probably never had a day go as planned. Leaders are confronted with constant challenges and obstacles throughout the day. The best leaders do not let these glitches fluster them, and they certainly do not let them ruin the day. They understand how to prioritize the challenges, and they take the unexpected snafus in stride. When the leader gets stressed, the other adults often get stressed. Conversely, when leaders respond to the challenges of the day with grace and a positive attitude, they help to set the tone for the day. They provide assurance to the other staff members, and they model constructive ways of dealing with adversity.

Remaining "positive" is not about always having a great day or a perfect attitude. We all have rough days. But it is about keeping things in perspective. And it is about an abiding certainty that we can choose to make a difference every day, in spite of the adversity. Tomorrow, we won't be able to control the weather, the attitudes of the kids, or the number of annoying emails that flood our inbox. But we can control the number of times we smile, the number of high-fives we give, and the energy we bring to work. We actually control a lot!

9

The Best Schools Make Decisions Based on the Needs and Passions of the Students, Not on the Interests and Traditions of the Adults.

Master schedules, teaching assignments, planning periods, grading practices, bell schedules, student seating arrangements, and a host of other decisions have to be made in the life of a school. In great schools, these decisions are not driven by convenience for the adults but by the needs of the students. What is best for the students? That is what we need to be doing. That is the question that should drive every decision. Great schools determine what is best for the students, and then they figure out how to make it happen. Sometimes it involves stepping outside of their comfort zone. Sometimes it involves thinking outside of the traditional schedule. Sometimes it requires creative problem solving. But the best schools find a way to make it happen.

10

Effective Leaders Do Not Focus on Making Good Decisions; They Focus on People. This Allows Them to Make Good Decisions.

Good leaders are not preoccupied with their position; they are preoccupied with their people. You cannot be a great principal if you do not love teachers. They do the core business of the school, and it is crucial that they feel valued and vital. So good leaders collaborate. Good leaders understand that the other adults in the building are the most important resource they have. They understand that you almost always make better decisions when you involve others in the process. Even the best leaders cannot solve all the problems. They do, however, engage others in a collective pursuit of solutions. When teachers are involved in the decision making process of the school, it makes it possible for them not just to support the mission of the school, but to *own* the mission of the school.

11

Every Hard Conversation in Your Building Is an Opportunity to Underscore the Core Values and Mission of Your School.

Very few leaders like confrontation. When principals need to address a problem, concern, or behavior with a teacher, those conversations can be awkward. I cannot imagine any leader who enjoys that part of the job – and actually, many leaders avoid those conversations all together. Maybe students have complained to the counselor that they often felt embarrassed by the teacher, and they are uncomfortable in the classroom. Maybe parents have called about a teacher who was not entirely professional during the parent conference. Maybe the administrator has observed the teacher interacting with challenging students in a manner that escalates rather than diffuses the situation. Are these concerns swept under the rug? Are they handled in a superficial way that simply allows the administrator to claim that they have "addressed the issue?"

These are important conversations and strong leaders find the courage to have them. These conversations are not simply about pacifying student complaints or parent complaints; they are opportunities to reinforce some important

values. Skilled administrators who understand the importance of supporting teachers will not begin any conversation
by accusing staff members; they will try to give them the
benefit of the doubt. But they will not shy away from
describing the perception of those who have concerns. And
they will place every conversation in the context of the
professional obligation of doing what's best for students.
Meeting the needs of students
must trump everything else in
the situation. Great administrators avoid making these conversations too personal; they try and
make them about the students.

> **"Meeting the needs of students must trump everything else in the situation."**

Every challenging conversation is an opportunity to remind
staff of our true purpose: Doing what is best for students.

12

There Is No Program That Is the Problem and There Is No Program That Is the Solution.

Flexible seating is one of the current trends in education – students standing up while working, sitting on exercise balls, or bean bag chairs. These have been very successful in the best teachers' classrooms. The students are respectful and understand how to behave appropriately as they move around the room independently.

Flexible seating can be a nightmare in a classroom that has not established expectations and mutual respect. Students race to the "cool seats," get in disputes over whose turn it is, and use these things as more of a disruption than a productive space.

"Clip up, clip down" is a highly effective classroom management technique in a calm, engaging, and consistent teacher's classroom. "Clip up, clip down" can make things worse if a teacher is volatile, inconsistent, or boring instructionally.

Intuitively we know this, but sometimes we lose sight of it. The best teachers are highly aware that is it what they do every day that determines their success. If flexible seating seems best for your students then by all means utilize it. However, if classroom management is a major struggle it may not be the answer. Our success as a teacher is determined by our relationships, appropriate expectations, and consistency. If we can do these three things then everything else we do will work out fine. If we cannot then there is no other solution. Programs are not the problem and programs are not the answer. The teacher is the determinant of what takes place in every classroom.

Principals have to support teachers as they make decisions. Rather than trying to add or eliminate programs on a school wide basis, school leaders must remember that supporting individual teachers can help provide the confidence for each staff member to be effective in their own way.

13

Teacher Morale Is Not Tricky. Involve Them. Support Them. Recognize Them. Value Them.

You may have heard it said, "We're here for the kids, not the teachers." You may have even said it. It's true. We *are* here for the kids. Students are the reason that schools exist, and every decision should be driven by the needs and interests of the children. However, do not make the mistake of thinking that student needs and teacher interests are mutually exclusive. I would actually argue that they are inextricably linked. To put it simply, happy teachers are more effective teachers. In fact, the morale of your faculty is an important component of a strong school culture.

Here is the good news: It is not that hard to raise the morale of your teachers! But it usually does not happen by accident – you must be intentional about it. Here are five ways you can raise the morale of your teachers:

1) Keep your teachers focused on the difference they are making for kids. Being a teacher is a profoundly gratifying career. It is easy to get bogged down in the administrivia though. The daily grind of planning lessons, grading papers, and dealing with the

more challenging students can sap the energy and joy from teachers. We need to remind our teachers why we come to work each day. We keep the focus on our students and not the "hassles" of the job. We remind our teachers about the difference that they make in the lives of their students. Our teachers are heroes in the classroom every day, and we never want to overlook that. When we help teachers keep their eye on the ball, they are more likely to keep their head in the game. When teachers remember their "why," it can carry them through the stresses of their day.

2) Involve your teachers in the decisions of the school. In my experience, teachers are more motivated when their administration leads collaboratively. When teachers are involved in the decisions of the school, they are more invested in the process. When their opinions are valued, *they* feel valued. Listen to the feedback of your teachers . . . and take it seriously. When teachers feel included in the decision making process, they will take ownership of the entire school, not just their classroom.

3) Trust the judgment of your teachers. Teachers are professionals. Treat them like professionals. Respect their experiences, and respect their expertise. Of course principals are responsible for the entire school and are ultimately accountable for everything that happens. But micromanagement is the quickest way to destroy the morale of a faculty. Give your teachers an opportunity to prove themselves. Good leaders will quickly learn which staff members require closer supervision.

4) Give your teachers the benefit of the doubt. Trust is foundational to any healthy school culture. When

you are frustrated with something a teacher said or did, assume that they had good intentions. Do not start off being judgmental. When your default setting is to give teachers the benefit of the doubt, it will not go unnoticed. Your teachers will feel supported, respected, and valued.

5) Notice the little things your teachers do ... and recognize them for it. It is not enough to think your team members are valuable; it is important to tell them. People need to know their work is appreciated, so praise your teachers often. Give them shout-outs in front of their colleagues. Thank them for the little things they do that make a difference for their students, for their colleagues, and for the school. Never underestimate the value of encouragement. Be specific, and be genuine. Never take your teachers, or the important work they do, for granted.

> "Never underestimate the value of encouragement. Be specific, and be genuine."

As teacher morale increases, so will the positive energy in the building. Students will notice it; parents will notice it; and anyone who visits the building will notice it. In my world, there is never a time when teacher morale is irrelevant. I strongly believe that teachers who feel good about coming to work, and who feel good about the work they do, will be more effective employees. They will bring a higher level of energy into the classroom, and they will demonstrate greater resiliency when confronted with adversity.

14

Our Job as Educators Is Not to Reflect Society. Our Job Is Much More Important than That — It Is to Cultivate Society.

There are so many demands of teachers. And they come from so many different directions. We need to teach basic skills. We need to teach life skills. We need to teach money management. We need to teach anti-bullying.

Someone does a study that shows people do not know enough U.S. history, so we blame the teachers. We do not know enough about world events, so we blame the school. Drug education, sex education, social media education ... whew, no wonder we are exhausted at the end of each day!

While all of these things seem important, they take a great deal of time and energy. That is a worry. However, a much greater concern is that they take us from the real mission of education. Our job is not to reflect society. We already have that. We have plenty of that. In certain areas we may have too much of that.

Instead our job as educators is actually to cultivate society. We need what we do not have. We need to help create new ideas and better people. We need each generation to be better than the previous one. We need to help develop a global perspective and one that also helps our community and neighborhoods.

We have to develop risk-takers. We have to enable young people to do new and better things. And one challenge is that often these breakthroughs will come from our "non-rule followers." They may not be the teacher-pleasers. Instead they

> **"** We have to develop risk-takers. We have to enable young people to do new and better things. **"**

may be the students that push back, question authority, and challenge our thinking. People that stay on the worn paths seldom discover new ground. We have to continually be aware of what is a primary purpose of schooling. To help improve each student and to help improve the world. That is one of the most challenging things educators do and one of the most fulfilling. Be a risk-taker and provide an environment in our schools to help students do the same Strong school culture is invaluable because it builds capacity . . . capacity to adapt and to grow. We don't know what the future holds, and we can't always predict what our students will need. But the right school culture will make it possible for us to rise to the challenge. It will be exciting to see what the next generation comes up with. Let's make sure we help it be the best it can be.

15

It Is Important That Educators Find Ways to Be Around Other Educators Who Are Equally Passionate about Their Job. We All Need to Be Encouraged, Inspired, and Validated in What We Do.

It is easy for educators to feel lonely and isolated in their profession. Teachers spend most of their day with students, and administrators also do not always have peers around whom they can identify with. It is essential that we all be intentional about connecting with other adults who are traveling our same path. For some of us, this means hanging out with colleagues in between classes, or maybe at lunch. For some of us, it means connecting with colleagues across the country through social media. These connections provide much-needed camaraderie, encouragement, and inspiration. When we engage with others who share our values, we are reminded of our own potential. This collegiality strengthens our professional pride, and the value of professional pride in the workplace cannot be overestimated. It is what compels us to be better today than we were yesterday. I thought I was a good principal until I began connecting with other school leaders on Twitter several years ago. When I saw what administrators around the country were doing in their schools, it opened my eyes to what was possible. It inspired me and encouraged me to elevate my game. Remember, peer pressure does not end with adolescence.

16

Students Do Not Always Follow Instructions . . . and Neither Do Teachers. We All Need to Be Patient with One Another.

The student did not bring the right book to class, and the teacher did not bring their laptop to the faculty meeting. The student was late to class because they were chatting with their friend. The teacher was late to their own class because they were out in the hallway conversing with a colleague. The student did not read all of the directions thoroughly on the test, and the teacher did not read the principal's email carefully – or at all. The student did not have their project turned in on time, and the teacher did not have their professional learning plan turned in on time.

Good teachers are gracious with their students. Good principals are gracious with their teachers. Loyal colleagues give one another the benefit of the doubt; they assume the best intentions. I cannot imagine anything more crucial to a school's culture than a foundation of trust – trust among the teachers, trust between teachers and students, and trust between the teachers and administration. It is an easy way to strengthen relationships. We all have flaws because, as it turns out, we are all human. But we should be patient with one another, and extend to one another a little bit of grace.

17

Management by Walking Around (MBWA) Is a Real Thing. There Is No Substitute for Visibility . . . and It Actually Facilitates More Effective Leadership.

Principals learn a great deal about their school by walking around. In the mornings, they learn whether the substitute has shown up. They learn if students are dressed appropriately. They see the students arguing and are able to prevent a fight. They notice the spill on the floor and are able to keep students from slipping. They notice the teacher who is rushing to make a couple of last-minute copies and are able to help cover their class. There is no way a leader can effectively manage the building from the confines of their office.

These management pieces certainly contribute to smoother operations in the building. But leaders should never underestimate the way in which MBWA enhances their leadership capacity. It communicates to all the staff and students that you are engaged – that you care about how things are going in the school. This level of engagement provides greater credibility to your leadership. You do not shape school culture in your office, and you certainly do not build it with emails and memos. You change culture through relationships ... one conversation at a time. You shape it in the halls, in the classrooms, in the lunchroom – engaging with those around you.

> " You change culture through relationships ... one conversation at a time. "

Great administrators walk around ... a lot. This is how they validate, how they recognize, how they communicate, and how they support. Walking around helps you manage your school; but it also helps you lead your school.

18

Innovative Teaching Does Not Happen in a Vacuum. It Happens in a Culture That Allows Teachers the Freedom to Fail. It Is a Culture of Trust.

Nobody likes to fail. We all want to feel competent, in control, and on top of our game. Teachers need to understand from their administrators, however, that there is not an expectation that every lesson will go perfectly. Teachers should not feel judged by their leaders when they are working through the "learning curve" of a new strategy or activity. Teachers always need the support and approval of their administrators, but this is especially true when they are experimenting with new professional practices.

Leaders must remember, however, that we will not encourage a culture of growth within our building if we are never willing to step outside of our own comfort zone. If we have not failed recently, we have not been trying anything new. If we want our teachers to innovate, we need to start by taking some risks ourselves. When things do not go as planned, be transparent about it. It may feel threatening, but there is strength in vulnerability. And teachers learn from our example. A school culture that values and celebrates innovation begins with a leader who is willing to climb out on a limb. You do not become awesome by staying safe all the time.

19

The Best Leaders Are Not the Ones With All the Good Ideas, They Are the Ones Who Figure Out How to Capitalize on the Good Ideas of Others.

Leaders cannot do it alone ... although insecure leaders sometimes try. Insecure leaders are driven by the need to feel adequate – to always be on top of their game. Strong leaders do not carry a grudge, and they are not burdened with the need to prove their leadership prowess. Rather, they seek to leverage the experiences, passion, and expertise among their staff. When teachers have cool ideas, good principals find ways for those teachers to "run with them." Good leaders don't have all the answers, but they're committed to finding them. They are comfortable with the reality that some of the best answers lie within the other adults in the building.

20

The Best Schools Recognize That the Staff Members Have Families, and Their Families Should Come before the Students.

Educators devote their entire careers to caring for other people's children. And great teachers take their job so personally, they often choose to attend to their children at work rather than their children at home. While it is good to be passionate about our vocations, and while it is admirable to be committed to your school and your students, we should always be mindful of the fact that we have jobs to support our own families. We strive for excellence in our careers, but we should never settle for mediocrity as a parent or a spouse. We all have families, and we need to take care of them. Teachers should never feel guilty about investing time in those they care the most about. And school leaders should explicitly communicate to staff members that families are a priority.

21

It Does Not Matter What You Claim to Care About; Everyone in the Building Knows What You Truly Care About by How You Spend Your Time.

Organizations take on the energy of their leader, so it is imperative that leaders continually project the core values that matter. And, when your values align with your actions, you are authentic. It is that simple.

So do you spend more time in your office or out in the hallways and classrooms? When you are in classrooms, are you there to evaluate and to judge, or are you there to engage and support? Do you spend more time responding to emails or talking to teachers? Do you spend more time filling out reports or interacting with students? Do you spend more time addressing the problems of the school or celebrating the successes of the school? Authentic leaders don't have to talk about their core values; everyone already knows their core values based on their actions. Great leaders spend their time and energy on the things that matter most.

Culture is not primarily built through mission statements, faculty meetings, and school improvement plans, but rather cultivated through hundreds of little interactions every day. I have heard of leaders having personal mission statements. Those can be a good thing, I guess … but great leaders do not actually need them – everyone in the building knows what they are about. Their values and priorities are consistently reflected in how they spend their time. The behavior of the principal is never neutral with respect to school culture. Like it or not, they build it every day. I don't want to build it accidentally or inadvertently; I want to build it on purpose.

One of the most valuable practices I ever started as a principal was when I began connecting with students on their birthday and taking "birthday selfies with the principal." When it's your birthday in our school, you get a shout-out on the intercom, and then at some point during the day, I will pull you out of class, wish you happy birthday, have a quick conversation, and take a selfie with you. I then text the picture to your mom or dad. Yes, this can sometimes take a lot of time –and no, taking selfies with students is not always convenient. But I cannot think of a better use of my time then connecting with kids on their special day. I want all our students to know that I care about them, and I want our teachers to know that our kids are always my priority. Make no mistake about it; others in the building will learn what we value by how we spend our time. I do not ever want there to be any ambiguity about what I value. The best mission statements are not framed; they are lived.

22

Great Principals Do Not Act Important; They Make Their Teachers Feel Important.

The role of the principal can never be overstated. Their impact is like a rock hitting a pond. The ripples continue endlessly. They have a tremendous influence on the culture and climate of the school. They can affect the morale of the students but they always directly affect the morale of the teachers.

Great principals treat their teachers the same way the best teachers treat their students. They make everyone feel important and valued. They do not treat everyone the same but they treat them all fairly. They listen, they laugh, and they build them up. *cheerleader for teachers*

When a principal makes the teachers feel important, the teachers make the students feel important. The principals know the key to the quality of the school is directly related to the quality of the teachers. The teachers are the most precious commodity in a school. Great principals know it and show it every day.

23

If a Principal Wants to Lose Their Teachers Quickly, They Should Brag About Themselves. If They Want to Build Relationships with Their Teachers, They Should Brag About Them.

The very best teachers have a consistent focus on their students. They make decisions based on what is best for the students and for the class. They never lose sight of that. Even if state standards, testing, and other mandates seem to take us down a different path, the best teachers quickly refocus on what is best for the students. They make everything they do about supporting, encouraging, and helping the young people in their class maximize their potential. They do not just do it for some of the students – they do it for all of the students.

The parallel between teachers and their students is incredibly similar to that of principals and their teachers. The very best principals have a consistent focus on their teachers. This does not mean that they lose sight of being student centered. Instead, it is because they know the best way to take care of their students is to take care of their teachers.

There are highly effective teachers that have larger than life personalities. There are highly effective teachers that work hard to stay out of the spotlight. Yet, regardless of their personal traits, all of the most effective teachers consistently center on the students.

This same thing is true for the best principals. Some are more outgoing than others, but all still work to make sure their teachers are "the main thing." They give credit and take blame. They protect the teachers from outside influences as much as possible, while simultaneously supporting them in their individual efforts.

The characteristics between the best teachers and the best principals have tremendous overlap. They both know what the ultimate goal is and are highly aware that they are only one piece of the puzzle. The best teachers know it is all about the students, and the best principals are highly aware of the essential role the teachers play in the success of any school. And in the best schools, the teachers and the administration are invested in the success of one another. They respect each other, and they appreciate each other, because they realize that they are all in it for the same reason: The KIDS!

24

We Would Like Parents to Be Involved at School, But We Need Parents to Be Involved at Home.

Recently I was involved in a Twitter chat where educators where discussing ways to increase parental (family) involvement with schools. There were many suggestions, some simple and others that seemed quite complex. To me the first key to increasing parental involvement with schools is to make sure every student has really good teachers. If there is a positive student–teacher relationship then parents are so much more likely to want to be involved in schools. If the students come home in a positive frame of mind related to school, there is much more likelihood of student success.

We must also remember that a parent not coming to open house night may have more to do with their personal burden than it does with their opinion of education. We cannot get caught up in the student's school needs and lose sight of the issues parents face each day. This is not to be used as an excuse, but to build an understanding.

Inversely, if a student is not having a good school experience it is much more difficult to have a positive family–school relationship; however, the aim is still to improve our interactions. The thing we must have for student success is parental involvement at home. This does not let educators off the hook. It instead means we should not lose sight of the significance of building relationships, so that we can help parents understand the importance of their involvement – the importance of reading to their child, for example. Providing a loving and caring family–school relationship could involve communicating ideas to help overburdened parents cope and being sensitive to the environment at home when assigning homework or how we handle correspondence.

Obviously the element of this we must first focus on is making sure every child has a really good teacher. That is where it has to start. We can never use the home environment as an excuse; instead we must first make sure that we take care of the school and educational environment. Parents send us the best children they have and they do the best they know how.

25

Schools Need to Do a Better Job of Recognizing Students who Are Not on the Honor Roll. There Are So Many Things that Matter Other than Grades.

There are some students in our schools that are discouraged. They do not feel like they fit in. They do not feel like they measure up. This is what I would like to tell them:

You are discouraged. I know you are. Your heart sank when you saw the grade. But that grade does not define you. You did your best ... but no one knows, and no one seems to care. You studied ... but your teacher does not think so. She does not know what happened at your house last night. She does not know why you did not get much sleep.

You have never made the honor roll, but you have worked harder for your "C" than some of those other kids worked for their "A." You are kind, but the teacher does not have a rubric for kindness. You smile every morning, but facial expressions do not go in the grade book. You gave a pencil to your classmate, but that did not earn you any points. You are always on time, and you are never in trouble, but there was not a question on the test about that. I am sorry we care so much about that grade. It certainly does not represent your hopes, goals, and dreams. I am sorry you were embarrassed when the teacher handed the papers back. You are gonna be fine. You have potential that is not measured by that last test. You have gifts that were not assessed by that last quiz. You did not make the honor roll, but I still think you are an awesome person with unlimited potential.

You are bored, and it is hard for you to care about assignments that do not have anything to do with your life. You are good at things the teacher does not seem to care about. You are passionate about things that are not on the syllabus. You are tired of being compared to those around you. You feel like you do not measure up – like you are inadequate. But your grade does not reflect your IQ or your worth. It is arbitrary. I am sorry that the grade is so important to all the adults. After you graduate, no one will care about that grade. They will care if you work hard; they will care how you work with other people; they will care about many things ... but they will not ask you about your GPA. You may not feel like a good student, but you will be a valuable employee. You will be a wonderful neighbor. You will be a great citizen.

You are discouraged ... but I want you to know I care. I want you to know I believe in you. I want you to know that you have a bright future. You have talents and gifts that we may not even know about yet. We have not found out how to measure them.

But you have them.

One size does not fit all, and I am sorry we have not figured that out. You are amazing ... and your worth will never be encapsulated by a grade. So please do not give up. Albert Einstein said, "If you judge a fish on its ability to climb a tree, it will live its whole life believing it is stupid." I am sorry you feel so judged. I am sorry we keep giving you trees to climb. If you're a fish, forget about the tree – just keep swimming.

26

A Collaborative Faculty Is Worth More than a School Improvement Plan ... But Principals Cannot Mandate Collaboration. The Goal Then, Is to Create the Conditions Where Teachers See the Value ... and Have the Time.

The best schools are characterized by faculties that are collaborative. The teachers meet regularly to discuss students, curriculum, instruction, and assessments. More than anything, this collaboration is the best way to improve professional practice. It provides the context in which teachers motivate each other to raise the bar. There are some teachers down the hall who have awesome ideas. They need to be stolen. That is what good teachers do ... they steal (they call it borrowing if they feel too guilty) awesome ideas wherever they can find them. A culture of collaboration ensures that teachers benefit from the experiences and expertise of colleagues. And learning from colleagues is often more meaningful than sitting in workshops, and

> **"**Collaboration is the best way to improve professional practice.**"**

positive peer pressure from colleagues is usually more meaningful than supervisory pressure from administrators.

Principals can send out emails about the importance of collaboration, but teachers can delete those emails. Principals can put memos about professional learning community guidelines in the mailboxes, and they can end up in the bottom of a pile on the teacher's desk. Principals can tout the value of peer coaching at a faculty meeting, and teachers can sit there quietly, composing their grocery list on their phone. It is important for school leaders to recognize that "best practices" are not implemented as a result of mandates; they are implemented because teachers believe in them and because they are supported and empowered to implement them.

So principals cannot force meaningful collaboration, and it certainly does not happen in a vacuum. But it can thrive when leaders create the right culture. Leaders need to highlight and celebrate the unique strengths of teachers. Leaders need to create a safe environment, so teachers understand it is ok to be vulnerable; it is ok to learn from colleagues. And leaders need to create school schedules that give teachers time together during the work day.

There are several things that we have done in our school to foster collaboration. We ran a year-long competition called "Collaboration Bling," where teachers earned bling through observing a colleague, through inviting a colleague to observe them, or through participating in a "Twitter chat." We have also experimented with different faculty meeting formats to give teachers a "voice" and allow them to more freely share ideas with colleagues. One meeting was conducted as a Twitter chat where all teachers reflected on goals and challenges via Twitter. We also conducted a faculty meeting "Edcamp" style by allowing teachers to generate the agenda and control the discussion. In this faculty meeting, our teachers provided the following topics: *"Dealing with parents," "Google Classroom," "Managing student cell-phone use in the classroom," "Incorporating writing in daily lessons,"* and *"Formative assessments."* The teachers had about 7 minutes to discuss their topic, and then I told them to rotate. In my experience, a culture of collaboration is the best formula for professional development out there. Learning from colleagues is more meaningful than sitting in workshops, and it is the principal's job to promote a culture within the school where collaboration becomes the norm.

27

Our Goal Should Be to Catch Teachers Being Awesome ... and Celebrate It. What Gets Validated Is What Gets Replicated.

Managers stop by to make sure teachers are working. Leaders stop by to encourage teachers in their work. Principals who adopt a "gotcha" mentality while they walk through their school undermine trust with faculty members and destroy the morale of teachers. Principals should spend far more energy catching their teachers doing the right thing than doing the wrong thing. Never miss an opportunity to brag about your colleagues to the visitors in the building – and preferably do so in front of the colleagues. Positive reinforcement goes a long way in promoting the professional behaviors that characterize great schools.

These "shout-outs" don't have to be for big things. Teachers make our schools great when they do the little things. Recognize these teachers:

The teacher who works tirelessly to prepare students for the real world.
The teacher who is committed to identifying what is in the best interest of their students.

The teacher who is passionate about learning new and improved ways of doing their job.

The teacher who has a passion for supporting their students that does not stop at 3:00pm.

The teacher who is willing to talk to students who are struggling.

The teacher who is willing to implement any strategy or activity in their classroom if it will make learning experiences more meaningful for their students.

The teacher who takes time to read to their students.

The teachers who routinely teaches bell to bell.

The teacher who embraces the challenge of reaching the students who seem the most unreachable.

The teacher who gets excited when they find a creative way to teach their lesson.

The teacher who instills pride in their students by consistently showing off their work.

The teacher who goes the extra mile to help their students be successful.

The teacher who is always in the hall in between classes.

The teacher who understands the power of respecting their students.

The teacher who works hard to be a positive role model for their students.

The teacher who refuses to let anything get in the way of their students learning.

The teacher who is always committed to rising above adversity.

The teacher who understands the importance of celebrating the successes of their students.

The teacher who utilizes every resource possible in pursuit of excellence in their classroom.

The teacher who is always willing to help out with things that aren't even in their job description.
The teacher who takes time to write personal notes on the papers they return to their students.

And it is not just the teachers who are doing great things in our schools! The support staff deserve our recognition as well.

The registrar who takes the time to show new students around the school.
The custodian who takes pride in how clean the floors are.
The cafeteria worker who takes time to talk to the students while they are serving food.
The secretary who is kind, patient, and helpful to all those who visit the building.
The paraprofessional who demonstrates extraordinary flexibility as they work to help everyone in the building.
The School Resource Officer who takes time to get to know the students.
The bookkeeper who brings extraordinary efficiency to their job to ensure that teachers have the resources they need as quickly as possible.
The nurse who understands that stomach aches are often more about stress than germs.
The maintenance technician who maintains a positive attitude even when they're being pulled in a million directions.
The media center specialist who will drop what they're doing to go and help a teacher who is having some "technical difficulties."
The counselor who goes above and beyond to connect students with resources to meet their needs.

28

The Greatest Joy Is Not Found in Our Ability to Improve Our Own Life, But in Our Ability to Improve the Lives of Others.

There's a scene in the movie *As Good as it Gets* where Melvin (the Jack Nicholson character) insults Carol (the Helen Hunt character) by ridiculing the dress she wore to the restaurant. Carol threatens to leave the restaurant unless Melvin pays her a compliment. After much consternation, he finally says, "You make me want to be a better man." As Carol melts in her chair, she responds, "That may be the best compliment of my life." That is one of my all-time favorite movie lines. It speaks to the potential we all have to bring out the best in other people.

There is value in being introspective, to be sure. We can grow personally and professionally through a strategic awareness on our own strengths and weaknesses. However, it is easy to become so self-absorbed that we miss out on opportunities to impact other people. It should be our goal to inspire those around us to become the best versions of themselves. And, frankly, when we are focused on improving the lives of others, many of our own problems do not seem as significant.

29

Great Schools Are Not Just Led by the Administration; They Are Led by Teachers Too. In Great Schools *Everyone* Owns the Vision . . . and *Everyone* Is on a Mission.

Most schools have a mission statement – maybe a vision statement too. It is probably on the school's website. It may be in a nice frame, hanging in the front office. Those mission statements are meaning*less* until the passionate educators in the school make them meaning*ful*.

In effective schools, the teachers don't just support the mission, they embrace it; they own it. They don't just show up for work to go through the motions or to jump through some hoops. They are passionate about making a difference for the students they serve. They are committed to making the words in the frame become a reality in the hallways, in the gym, in the cafeteria, and in the classrooms.

Every school has a principal; many schools have one or more assistant principals as well. This administrative team leads the school. But in effective schools, they're not the *only* ones leading the school. They are not lone rangers, secluded in their office, calling all the shots, and presuming to have all the answers. They collaborate with the faculty and involve the teachers in the decision making process. The teachers have a stake in everything that happens; they feel vested in the process. The principals do not assume sole responsibility for the direction of the school, and the teachers are not passive in the process of moving the school forward. They feel empowered to bring their own ideas, their own talents, and their own voice to the table. And effective administrators are secure enough to give them that voice.

30

Sometimes the Difficulty of the Climb Has More to Do with the Attitude of the Climber than It does the Altitude of the Peak.

Our jobs are challenging. They take a tremendous level of energy. They take a daily commitment in order to be effective. A big part of this is that we want to make sure that what we do provides a positive difference and has great impact and importance. This can become overwhelming.

Every year we start excited and become exhausted. On days when we begin with high energy we still often feel drained. We give and we give ... and, at times, we get back. We see a student "get it" for the first time. Their eyes light up with excitement. It doesn't matter whether students are 5 or 18 – every time it happens we feel the same. It reminds us why we chose to teach. We remember that it is all worth it – that what we do has a timeless impact and our legacy lives on well beyond our years.

When we are able to recenter on why we chose education, when we can recall some of our most positive outcomes, when we reflect on the difference we make every day, that mountain can quickly become more climbable. And the hike definitely is worth it.

31

Skip the Email and Have a Personal Conversation Instead. You Do Not Build Trust and Relationships through Typing; You Build Them through Talking.

There is no doubt that email represents one of the most efficient forms of communication. But here's the thing: When you strive to cultivate a strong school culture, efficiency is not the goal; relationships are. Culture begins with relationships, and relationships begin with conversations. Schools with a healthy culture have adults that talk to one another. You do not usually build rapport via email. And, actually, emails can do some relational damage because of the potential for people to read tone into language and misunderstand the intent of the communication. Emails are a valuable form of communication to be sure, but never underestimate the importance of personal conversations. We all probably need to spend more time talking to one another.

What do you communicate through your conversations with the secretary ... with the custodian ... with the lunch supervisor?

While the teachers are the adults engaged in the core business of the school, it is a tragic mistake to underestimate the value and contributions of those individuals who play a supportive role. Most principals appreciate the work of the secretaries, custodians, and CNP staff, but they may not always be mindful of how their interactions with these people enhance the culture of the school. When you invest in your support staff, you demonstrate to all those around you that everyone in the school is valued. A strong relationship with your support staff goes a long way toward ensuring the school runs smoothly. It affects the morale of the teachers, and it certainly creates a more positive environment in the building.

> "When you invest in your support staff, you demonstrate to all those around you that everyone in the school is valued."

32

We Should Not Want New Teachers to Fall in Line – We Need New Teachers to Form New Lines.

Many educators are very proud of their schools. And they should be. We have so many wonderful things going on in education. It is truly amazing. And each year most schools have new faculty and staff members join the group. We want people to fit in to help us sustain the excellence that is taking place in our schools. However, it is important that we not lose sight of what energy and excitement new people can bring to an organization – even one that is already firing on all cylinders. They need to take us places we have never been before.

When we hire a new teacher our goal should be for our school to become more like the new teacher. In other words we need to hire what we need rather than what we have. Think of the excitement and optimism that new staff members have. They are going to change the world. And we should want them to. Once in a while a few teachers in some schools can become jaded and even negative. We do not want that to permeate a new teacher. Let's join their excitement and remember that level of enthusiasm that we have (or at least have had) within ourselves.

Rather than taking a cynical view toward the optimism of new teachers, let's bask in the sunshine they are providing. We can admire their energy and fearlessness and recall how we felt when we had our initial classroom full of students. Every school has a "welcoming committee" for new teachers – be it formal or informal. Some schools put great thought into designating and designing a group to help new staff segue into success. Others hope that the new staff members randomly align with the positive influencers in the school and somehow avoid the negative peers who might share a schedule with them. Either way, there is a welcoming committee, and we can decide whether we want it to happen randomly or not. Let's make sure ours has the same positive tone that the new teachers bring to us. We want to have a school where new teachers do not feel the need to defer to what is there. We want to welcome the new perspective and ideas that can help us all become even better.

Welcoming committee
ensures haters don't
have greater influence
Be intentional

33

There Are Few Things More Powerful than a Well-Placed Compliment.

Every time we give praise at least two people feel better – one of them is us. Let's reflect on that special teacher, friend, or relative that made us feel better whenever we were around them. We walked a little taller, felt a little prouder, and saw the world in a better light. Those are the type of people we want to be around and, most importantly, the type of people we want to be.

As leaders, not only is it better to behave in a positive fashion, it really should be a requirement. Part of what we have to do to be effective is to lift our students up. They deserve to feel valued and need to become confident. The best teachers do this on a consistent and regular basis. Others seldom take this approach.

Luckily, as educators we have the opportunity to practice this at home and at school. We need to always look for the good part, even if we have to squint. This does not replace the importance of helping students grow and improve – that is also essential – it just makes our ability to do so easier. When you feel like someone values you, you value them and their guidance so much more. We have to *build* a relationship before we *need* the relationship, and acknowledging people's positive traits, efforts, and actions can greatly increase our chances of influencing them in a positive direction. Encouraging words never get old. Ever. If you want to make a difference for someone, build them up with your words. They don't have to be special words, or profound words; they just have to be from the heart.

34

One of the Indicators of a Strong School Culture Is the Extent to Which Teachers Feel Ownership in the Entire School, Not Just Their Classroom.

Have you ever heard a staff member say, "That's not my problem?" Are teachers comfortable retreating into the isolation of their classroom and doing their own thing? Hopefully, not. The best faculties function as a team – as a cohesive unit. Teachers are invested in one another and in the success of the school. They understand that they are not my kids, your kids, or their kids; they are OUR kids.

35

Teachers Buy into the Principal before They Buy into the Principal's Vision. Do Not Underestimate the Relationships. Do Not Underestimate the Process.

Leadership is not about implementing programs; it is about connecting with people. Good leaders care more about their people than they do about their vision. A vision is important ... but the people always come first. Good principals bring out the best in their teachers. Those teachers are not driven to comply; they are inspired to grow. Principals cannot make teachers "buy in." The best leaders build relationships ... and then the teachers *choose* to buy in. And these relationships are not generated out of thin air; they are cultivated through conversations. There is no substitute for face to face interactions with teachers.

> "The best leaders build relationships ... and then the teachers *choose* to buy in."

Most principals have a vision for academic excellence in their school, and they have a good idea of what the teachers need to do to make that vision a reality. It is important for all administrators to recognize though that first and foremost teachers are not looking for "instructional leadership," they are looking for support. And, when they feel the support, they are much more receptive to the instructional leadership.

If you want to be a good leader, start by being good to the people you work with. They may not remember your ideas, your skill, or your vision, but they will always remember how you treated the people you worked with.

36

People Are Not Born Extraordinary; They Become Extraordinary When They Make the Decision Not to Settle for Average.

Excellence is what results from thinking "good enough" is never good enough. I fondly recall a staff member who was working on a project for me. She emailed me the finished product, but in her email, she said, "Let me know if it's not excellent because I'll redo it until it is excellent." I remember how inspired I was by the commitment of that colleague, and by the high standard that her comment reflected. Doing that little bit extra, going above and beyond – that is what it takes to be excellent. Educators who are extraordinary became that way by making lots of little decisions to rise above mediocrity.

37

Do Not Just Focus on Test Scores – Focus on Student Engagement. When You Get that Right, the Test Scores Will Take Care of Themselves.

Make no mistake about it, student achievement is important. More often than not, that is how the public will judge the success of our schools. It is important for us to always remember, however, that student achievement does not happen in a vacuum. It happens in a cultural context where students are inspired and teachers are empowered. It happens when teachers have maximized their instructional efficacy through professional collaboration. It happens when the adults share a common commitment to connecting with the students in the building. It happens when the adults work to ensure all the students feel valued and supported. Student achievement is often a function of student engagement, and student engagement is much more likely when the students feel emotionally safe.

38

There's a Difference between "Complaining" and Identifying Challenges. The Best Teammates Are Always Looking for Solutions.

One teacher told me, "I see students walking all over school listening to their phones or playing one of their games. These kids don't listen, and they don't care about the rules. So I've stopped saying anything to them." Another teacher told me, "We might need to revisit our guidelines for cell-phone use. I've noticed it is becoming more of a distraction." Hopefully, you see the difference in tone between those two statements. When staff members complain, they are doing little more than injecting negative energy into the situation. They are exasperated; they are venting; and they are not trying to solve any problems. Staff members who stay positive are not "Pollyanna," naive, or looking through "rose-tinted glasses." They are simply committed to remaining constructive. Every school has problems. Even good schools have challenges. The thing about good schools is that they tackle those challenges in a constructive way. They do not just complain about the challenges, they look for solutions. Rather than thinking it cannot be done, they think: "I cannot wait to figure out how we are going to do it."

39

Great Culture Is Possible When the Adults in the School Share the Same Core Values . . . and Make Decisions Based on Them.

Good school culture is not accidental, and it is not the result of a lot of gimmicks. It is not rocket science either. It is mostly a matter of all the adults in the building staying mindful of why they come to work – of why they do what they do. It results from educators who love their job and make decisions based on the best interests of students. It results when all the adults in the building are motivated to do what is best for kids. One of the best things about school culture is that everyone gets to contribute to it. It is not just a reflection of the administration or the leadership team; it is a reflection of everyone. And you can transform your school's culture for free. It doesn't cost anything to focus on the students. It doesn't cost anything to collaborate. And it doesn't cost anything to keep a positive attitude.

40

When Administrators Spend Time in Classrooms, They Are Reminded How Much Teachers Have to Plan, How Much They Have to Manage, and How Unbelievably Patient They Are.

It takes a lot of time to develop engaging lessons. It takes a lot of energy to stay upbeat for all the students. It takes a lot of patience to handle some of the struggling and challenging students. When principals visit classrooms on a regular basis, they communicate to teachers that their work is valued. In the classrooms, they get to experience instructional highlights, but they also get to witness instructional challenges. Administrators always have greater credibility when the teachers know they are aware of the realities in the classroom. Teachers are the heart and soul of every school, and the best way to connect with them is to watch them in their element – the classroom.

41

Good Leaders Focus on the Right Stuff. Great Leaders Remember That the Right "Stuff" Is Always People.

You are busy! You have a lot of things on your to do list. It would be so tempting to be frustrated with the constant interruptions. But never underestimate your ability to make someone's day by how you respond to those little distractions – the ones you could easily view as an annoyance. You never know which moments with people will be the ones that they remember ... potentially for a long time. So embrace the interruptions. Make the most of those unplanned, unscheduled moments. They could end up being the most important moments of your day.

42

If You're an Administrator Don't Assume Your Teachers Know You Support Them. You Gotta Show Them . . . Every Day.

How many times have you signed off on an email to the staff by saying: "Thanks for all you do!" I know I have written those words. Don't get me wrong, that's not a bad thing to say to a staff. But as administrators, we need to be about more than words. We can't just talk about the faculty being a family; we have to act like it is a family. We can cover their class so they can run off campus to see their own child's program. We can check on them when they have been out sick. We can spend time watching them teach – not to evaluate them, just to support them. As leaders, we need to do more than just talk about supporting our teachers; we want our behavior to reflect that priority. When teachers show their care for students on a regular basis, it makes it a good place for them to learn. When administrators support the teachers on a regular basis, it makes it a good place to work.

43

Leaders Should Never Underestimate the Value of Imagination. Dreaming About What Could Be Is the First Step in the Process of Unlocking Organizational Potential.

Robert Kennedy once said, "There are those who look at things the way they are, and ask 'why?' I dream of things that never were, and ask 'why not?'" I love this quote because it reflects a commitment to rising above the status quo, to shattering barriers, and to envisioning new opportunities.

I remember showing our counselor a short video online called, "Strangers in a Ball Pit." It is a heartwarming clip of how strangers can bond and develop a friendship while talking with one another in a ball pit. Immediately after watching this 7-minute video, our counselor indicated that we needed one for our school. We started to brainstorm about how it might be used for things like peer mediation, grief therapy, and working through anxiety. The possibilities seemed endless. But what a far-fetched idea! Who would construct this ball pit, or where would we even get one? How would we pay for it? We don't have room for this! Where would we put it? Would central office even approve it? No question about it ... this was not a practical idea.

But what if? If we could figure out a way to make this happen it would be ridiculously awesome! And I heard my own mom say hundreds of times: "Where there's a will, there's a way." So ... our central office helped us purchase building supplies. A local church helped us purchase the balls. And our unbelievably talented maintenance technician constructed the coolest ball pit you've ever seen. So we now have a ball pit at our school that the students love. There were a myriad of reasons that this couldn't or shouldn't happen, but we pushed through. And I am so glad we did.

44

Micromanagement Can Sometimes Ensure Adequacy ... but It Rarely Fosters Excellence.

When the goal is compliance, vigilant supervision is a priority. When an administrator wants to ensure that teachers are dotting all their "i's" and crossing all their "t's," looking over their shoulder can be an effective management strategy. Micromanagement is perhaps the most logical approach to ensure that the employees are doing what the boss expects.

But here's the catch: This type of management style will likely only yield the bare minimum performance from the employee. Moreover, it fails to account for a primary function of leadership: Creating the conditions for excellence. Teachers who feel micromanaged by their principal will not take risks; they will not grow; they will not innovate; and, more than likely, they will never reach their potential. Why? They are too busy trying to avoid mistakes. They are too worried about what their boss will think. Furthermore, when teachers perceive that they are micromanaged by their administration, the trust that should exist in a healthy administrator–teacher relationship is undermined – and this sabotages staff morale. It is certainly the principal's responsibility to hold teachers accountable for doing their job, but it should be done in the context of a trusting relationship. Effective principals have confidence in their staff to do their job. They respect the professional judgment of their teachers, and this increases the likelihood that those teachers will pursue excellence in their classrooms.

> " Effective principals have confidence in their staff to do their job. "

When you are a manager, people do the right thing when you're looking. When you are a leader, people do the right thing even when you're not looking.

45

Administrators Should Be Inspired by the Teachers in Their Building ... If They're Not They Need to Figure Out a Different Way to Lead.

Every school has teachers who form amazing connections with students. Every school has teachers who develop creative and engaging lessons. Every school has teachers who exert a little bit of positive peer pressure on their colleagues because of their commitment to collaboration. Every school has teachers who bring positive energy into the building simply because of their relentless commitment to making a difference for students. These are the qualities that define great educators and they remind us why we come to work each day.

Principals, you have these teachers in your building, and they should inspire you every day. If they don't, maybe you're not paying close enough attention to the work that is going on in the classrooms. Maybe you are taking some of the amazing work of your teachers for granted. If you feel like there is not a lot of "amazing work" going on, maybe you should look in the mirror. Maybe there is something you can do differently to create a culture that fosters amazing work. Maybe you should spend more time encouraging your teachers and praising them for the work they do. As a principal, to a large degree, your teachers will be a reflection of you. If you are not inspired by the reflection, it might be a good idea to evaluate your own work. Principals want teachers to reflect on their lessons, and they need to be willing to reflect on their leadership.

46

Teachers Don't Need Anything Else on Their Plates ... And Good Administrators Never Lose Sight of How Heavy Those Plates Can Be.

We ask a lot of our teachers. They need to teach state mandated courses of study with innovative, scaffolded, and engaging lessons. We want them to individualize their instruction and remain mindful of the variety of accommodations that their students need. We want them to prepare their students to excel at high stakes, standardized tests. We expect them to form meaningful relationships with the students in their class. We ask them to communicate regularly with the parents and engage them in a meaningful way in their child's education. We ask them to teach "character" to their students and instill in them a sense of pride, integrity, kindness, empathy, and good work ethic. We ask them to give up their planning time to collaborate with their professional learning community. We ask them to stay late for faculty meetings and various committee assignments. We ask them to show patience and compassion toward some of the most challenging students imaginable. And we want them to show good school spirit – always bringing a positive attitude to work every day.

That's a lot to ask of our teachers. Yep ... we expect a great deal. Good administrators never lose sight of what is asked of teachers. They never lose sight of how high that bar is. They demonstrate empathy for their teachers and never take their hard work for granted. Good administrators understand the heavy load that teachers carry, and they look for small ways to lighten it. Teaching is hard work; it is a labor of love. While teachers did in fact sign up for this, they are profoundly grateful for administrators who understand the challenges, the pressures, and the commitments. They appreciate it when administrators can find ways to alleviate some of the pressure and help with some of the challenges. And they certainly are grateful for administrators who think twice before adding one more thing to the plate.

> "Good administrators understand the heavy load that teachers carry, and they look for small ways to lighten it."

47

It Is Difficult to Improve Student Achievement without First Improving School Culture.

Students are more involved in their own learning when they feel safe, valued, and connected. Teachers are more effective when they are working in a school where their professional judgment is trusted and their efforts in the classroom are validated. They are more motivated and more energized when the energy in the building is positive. Their instruction and assessments are more meaningful when they have the support and inspiration of their colleagues. If principals want to impact student achievement, it is incumbent on them to invest their energy in creating the type of school culture where both teachers and students are engaged in the educational process. Certain conditions are clearly more favorable than others for fostering student learning and increasing student achievement. Effective school leaders are focused on creating those conditions.

48

Organizations Feed Off the Energy of Their Leader – So Schools Need Principals Who Are Excited About What They Are Doing.

When you enjoy your job, everyone around you knows it. The authenticity is compelling ... and inherently engaging. And it is important that principals realize that their attitude affects the attitude of those they wish to lead. When principals are excited about leading, teachers are more likely to be excited about teaching, and students are more likely to be excited about learning. Good leaders are not remembered for their plans or their programs; they are remembered for their passion and their sense of purpose.

So what is the passion and purpose that drives good principals? They come to work each day to remove barriers for our teachers. They strive to create a safe school environment for students. They commit to leading a school where teachers want to work and students want to learn. They create a vision for our school community that encourages students to dream big and ensures teachers can help students achieve those dreams.

They remember that we actually play a role in raising student achievement. They embrace the responsibility of creating a school culture that elevates expectations for students and fosters meaningful collaboration among teachers. They sit with our teachers to analyze data, but they remember that each data point represents a student, their future, and all of their hopes and dreams. They work to increase student achievement, but they remember that they did not get into the business to raise test scores; they became educators to make a difference in the lives of their students.

They demonstrate every day through what they say and how they spend their time that meeting the needs of their students is the most important thing they do. They know that they have students walking their halls who need them. They advocate for the student who has been picked on. They are patient with the student who does not have any support at home. They make time for the student who is lonely. They are relentless about connecting with the students in their school, and they remind their teachers that they leave a legacy that transcends the curriculum. They remind them that students may not always remember their lesson, but they will always remember their kindness.

The job of a school principal is challenging – and at times it is certainly stressful. But they keep their focus. They keep their eye on the ball. They come to work every day to empower their teachers and inspire their students, to create for them a brighter future.*

Note

* A portion of this section appeared in a post by Danny Steele, originally published by NASSP's blog, "School of Thought."

Continue the Conversation

Which truths and anecdotes resonated with you the most? Share your thoughts and join the conversation with Danny Steele (@steelethoughts) and Todd Whitaker (@toddwhitaker) on Twitter using the hashtag #essentialtruths.